Sacrifice on the Somme

Michael Hall

ISLAND (2) PAMPHLETS

Published 1993 by Island Publications
132 Serpentine Road, Newtownabbey, Co Antrim BT36 7JQ

© Michael Hall

ISBN 0 9514194 3 9

With acknowledgements to:

The Farset Somme Project for access to their interviews with veterans.

The Somme Association for providing some of the photographs.

Dr Ian Adamson of Pretani Press for his sponsorship.

The Imperial War Museum for use of some of the photographs.

War Clouds

A few years before the First World War would plunge a whole generation of young men into a conflagration of unimagined proportions, the only 'war' that people in Ireland felt might be on the horizon was one brewing on their own doorstep. Asquith's Liberal government was intending to introduce a Home Rule Bill that would grant Ireland a limited measure of independence. The Protestants of Ulster, however, were making strenuous plans to oppose such a dissolution of the Union. Under the leadership of Sir Edward Carson, they began to organise on a massive scale. On 28 September 1912 almost half a million Ulster men and women signed a 'Solemn League and Covenant', pledging their willingness to fight to remain part of the United Kingdom. This preparedness to fight was reinforced in January 1913 with the formation of the Ulster Volunteer Force (UVF). All sections of Protestant society were now united and organised in a massive paramilitary force, working-class men training in the estates of the landed gentry.

The Nationalist population of Ireland naturally looked upon these preparations with grave misgivings. They were relying on the British government to deliver its promises, but in what way could the organised Ulstermen affect the issue? Some leading Nationalists endeavoured to see a positive side to events. Eoin MacNeill, founder of the Gaelic League, wrote: 'A wonderful state of things has come to pass in Ulster... The Ulster Volunteer movement is essentially and obviously a home rule movement. (It is) the most decisive move towards Irish autonomy that has been made since O'Connell invented constitutional agitation. It claims, no doubt, to hold Ireland 'for the Empire'; but really what matters is *by whom Ireland is to be held.*' [1]

A more pragmatic response to the Ulstermen's behaviour was the formation of the Irish National Volunteers. Ireland was girding its loins for the approaching collision. In March 1914 sixty officers of the British Army, stationed at the Curragh camp, stated that they would prefer to be dismissed rather than have to move against Ulster. In April the UVF managed to pull off a highly successful gun-running operation that provided them with 24,000 rifles and two million rounds of ammunition. The Irish Volunteers also ran a consignment of weapons into the country – 1,500 rifles and 40,000 rounds of ammunition. Ireland was fast becoming an armed camp. Then, on 4 August 1914, Britain declared war on Germany.

In Ireland loyalties, even at the best of times, have never been straightforward. Many Protestants wanted to fight for Britain, others were more concerned that the Ulster crisis was still undecided. Many Catholics wished to aid Britain, while others felt that England's difficulty was Ireland's opportunity. Many Unionists *and*

Oglaigh na hEireann.

ENROL UNDER THE GREEN FLAG.

Safeguard your rights and liberties (the few left you).

Secure more.

Help your Country to a place among the nations.

Give her a National Army to keep her there.

Get a gun and do your part.

JOIN THE

IRISH VOLUNTEERS

(President: EOIN MAC NEILL).

The local Company drills at_____

Ireland shall no longer remain disarmed and impotent.

Nationalists believed that loyalty to England in this hour of need would be rewarded politically when the war ended. 'We are not fighting to get away from England,' said Carson, 'we are fighting to stay with England. Our country and our Empire are in danger. I say to our Volunteers, go and help to save our country.' John Redmond, on behalf of the Nationalists, likewise declared their loyalty to the British government, but with different hopes – 'It is these soldiers of ours to whose keeping the Cause of Ireland has passed today.' [2] Thousands of Irish Volunteers were to enlist in existing Irish regiments or in the newly formed 10th and 16th Irish Divisions.

A few voices expressed scepticism about the British government's claims to be 'fighting for small nations'. The Irish Socialist James Connolly wrote in the *Irish Worker*: 'Should the working class of Europe, rather than slaughter each other for the benefit of kings and financiers, proceed tomorrow to erect barricades all over Europe, to break up bridges and destroy the transport service that war might be abolished, we should be perfectly justified in following such a glorious example, and contributing our aid to the final dethronement of the vulture classes that rule and rob the world.' [3]

But from all over the island, Irishmen, Protestant and Catholic, Northerner and Southerner, came forward in their thousands to enlist. In some towns the Ulster Volunteers and the Irish Volunteers marched side by side to send off departing troops.

Kitchener, the Secretary of State for War, made it clear he wanted the Ulster Volunteers for his 'New Army', and met with Carson. Carson won the argument to keep the UVF together as a unit, and the 36th (Ulster) Division was born. As for the Home Rule Bill, it was to be kept inoperative for the duration of the war.

Within four years the number of Ulstermen and Irishmen who were to give their lives totalled 50,000. But before that, Ulster Protestants in the 36th (Ulster) Division and Irish Catholics (including many from Ulster) in the 16th (Irish) Division were to shed their blood together near a river in France – the Somme.

Ulster Volunteers in training, 1914

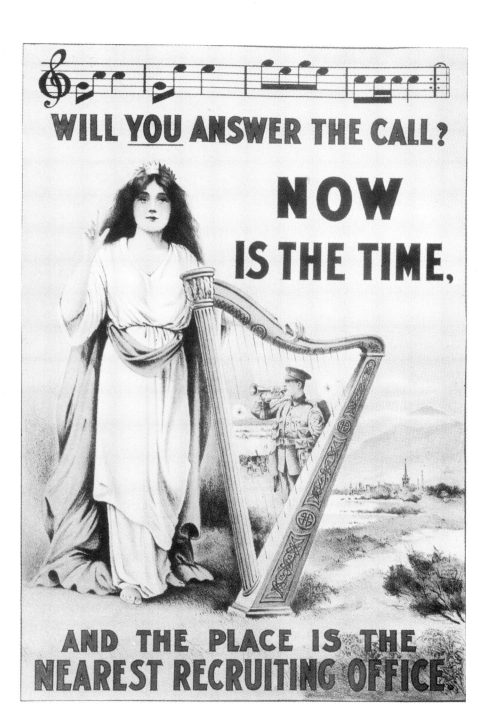

The Road to the Somme

When the First World War began it was greeted in the participating countries with a fervour and enthusiasm that at times bordered on hysteria. All the nations involved believed in the righteousness of their cause – the French were fighting for *la patrie*, the Germans for the Fatherland, the Russians for Holy Mother Russia, and the British for 'a war to end war'. It would be, so many imagined, a spectacle of great and glorious battles, above all a war of 'movement'. And as for its duration, some even believed it might well be over by Christmas. Few could have suspected what a devastating war of attrition it would become, a war for which memorials to the dead would have to be erected in almost every town and village in Europe, memorials to the real heroes of the conflict, the 'lost generation' of unknown soldiers.

The reality of how the war would unfold quickly became apparent. A French offensive in Lorraine against the German flank was a disaster. The French suffered terrible casualties and reeled back in confusion and disorder. They lost the flower of their armies, a loss from which they never fully recovered. To the north, the Germans advanced through Belgium almost unimpeded. The British Expeditionary Force clashed with them at the mining town of Mons on 23 August 1914, and although the BEF did well in the engagement they had to retreat because of their precariously exposed flanks.

But the Germans, who had advanced to within thirty miles of Paris, had also overstretched themselves. Realising the danger this left them in, they began a general retreat. As A.J.P. Taylor described it:

> On 14 September the Germans reached the Aisne. They were exhausted, could march no more. [They] scratched holes in the ground, set up machine guns. To everyone's amazement, the advancing Allies hesitated, stopped. The campaign was over. One man with a machine gun, protected by mounds of earth, was more powerful than advancing masses. Trench warfare had begun. The war of movement ended when men dug themselves in. They could be dislodged only by massive bombardment and the accumulation of reserves. Indeed they did not move at all. The opposing lines congealed, grew solid. The generals on both sides stared at these lines impotently and without understanding. They went on staring for nearly four years.'[4]

1915 only saw more confirmation of this state of affairs. On the Western Front attack and counter-attack followed one after the other, with little gain in territory but an ever-lengthening casualty list. Further afield the Allied assaults at Gallipoli and Salonika became bogged down just as surely as in the mud of France.

A French soldier pays the price

On the Eastern Front there was at least a war of movement, but one with just as terrible a cost. A combined German and Austro-Hungarian offensive on 2 May blew the Russian front wide open. The Russians 'lost three-quarters of a million men in prisoners alone, and more territory than the whole of France. Something like ten million civilian refugees trailed along with the armies.' [4] As the Russians fell back, the German advance slowed, and Russia somehow managed to remain in the war.

In 1916 the Allied Commanders began to feel more confident. The citizens of the British Isles had flocked to enlist, and gradually Kitchener's New Armies in France grew into a mighty force. The British Commander-in-Chief, General Sir Douglas Haig, wanted an offensive in Flanders, but his French counterpart, General Joffre, pointed instead to the Somme, where the British and French lines joined. There was little of strategic importance to be gained here, but Joffre wanted to pull the British into heavy fighting alongside the French.

However, while the Allies made their plans, the Germans struck. General Falkenhayn, the German Chief of Staff, was aware of the great losses suffered by the French. If he could inflict a death blow that forced them out of the war, the British would have to accept a compromise peace. The target was to be Verdun, a famous fortress town of great symbolic importance to French pride. It stood at the head of a precarious salient in the French line, and, unknown to the French people, had already been stripped of most of its guns.

> Falkenhayn calculated that France would be forced to defend this semi-sacred citadel to the last man. By menacing Verdun with a modest outlay of only nine divisions, he expected to draw the main weight of the French army into the salient, where German heavy artillery would grind it to pieces from three sides. In Falkenhayn's own words, France was thus to be 'bled white'. It was a conception totally novel to the history of war and one that, in its very imagery, was symptomatic of that Great War where, in their callousness, leaders could regard human lives as mere corpuscles.' [5]

The bombardment began at dawn on 21 February, and continued for nine hours. The bombardment was of an intensity the world had never seen. The poorly prepared French trenches were pulverised, many of the defenders being buried alive. Briand, the French Prime Minister, rushed to consult his officers. Many of them felt they would be better off without Verdun, but Briand, losing his temper, exclaimed that there could be no thought of surrendering the fortress. The French had fallen into Falkenhayn's trap.

The French defended Verdun heroically, but at terrible cost, not just in casualties, but for the French fighting spirit. Yet Falkenhayn's plan had backfired, for while he had only wished to slaughter Frenchmen by artillery fire, German prestige now demanded that German troops too be fed into this cauldron of death.

Joffre sent an agonised appeal to his allies. Haig agreed to bring the Somme offensive forward from 1 August to 1 July. On the Eastern Front the Russians returned to the offensive, and General Brusilov managed to forge a remarkably successful breakthrough, taking a quarter of a million prisoners in three weeks. But the Russians had no reserves, and had to retreat under the German counter-attack, suffering over a million casualties.

At Verdun the fighting continued unabated and the casualties mounted on both sides. On 23 June German machine-gun bullets were striking the town streets. There were ominous signs that French morale was cracking. How much more could they take?

Two days later, the sound of British heavy guns was heard in Verdun. Haig's five-day bombardment on the Somme had begun.

The Realities of War

Before we discuss the Battle of the Somme, we should look at what trench warfare entailed. When, on 25 September 1915, the French attacked in the region of Champagne they made an alarming discovery: 'Though they overran the German front line, this brought no advantage. The Germans had a fully prepared second line behind it. The original thin trenches were, in fact, growing thicker: the front held by fewer men, the real defence stronger behind it and easier to reinforce. This defence in depth turned ordinary offensives into pointless slaughter.' [4]

The German defences which the British troops would attack were a formidable and foreboding obstacle. As General Haig described them:

> The enemy had spared no pains to render the defences impregnable. The first and second systems each consisted of several lines of deep trenches, well provided with bomb-proof shelters, and with communication trenches. The front of the trenches in each system was protected by wire entanglements, many of them in two belts forty yards broad, the barbed wire often as thick as a man's finger. The numerous woods and villages in and between these systems of defence had been turned into veritable fortresses. The deep cellars and numerous pits were used to provide cover for machine guns and trench mortars, and these were supplemented by elaborate dug-outs, sometimes in two storeys and connected by passages sometimes as much as thirty feet below the surface. The salients in the enemy's line, from which he could bring enfilade fire across his front, were made into self-contained forts, and often protected by mine-fields; while strong redoubts and concrete machine gun emplacements had been constructed in positions from which he could sweep his own trenches should these be taken. The ground lent itself to good artillery preparation on the enemy's part, and he had skilfully arranged for cross-fire by his guns.' [6]

A Russian soldier searches among his dead comrades

Not all the defences were so intricate or thorough. The French forward lines at Verdun were nowhere near as adequate or as deep, and the French soldiers paid the price for this deficiency. The slaughter caused by the bombardment was horrible in its intensity. One soldier recalled how 'the shells disinterred the bodies, then reinterred them, chopped them to pieces, played with them as a cat plays with a mouse.'

And those still living had to watch, wait and endure. 'One eats, one drinks beside the dead, one sleeps in the midst of the dying, one laughs and sings in the company of corpses', wrote Georges Duhamel, poet and dramatist. The waiting itself was nerve-wracking. Paul Dubrulle, an infantry sergeant who was later killed, wrote:

> The most solid nerves cannot resist for long; the moment arrives where the blood mounts to the head; where fever burns the body and where the nerves, exhausted, become incapable of reacting ... finally one abandons oneself to it, one has no longer even the strength to cover oneself with one's pack as protection against splinters, and one scarcely still has left the strength to pray to God. [5]

Even when not under fire, life was far from pleasant. Cyril Falls wrote:

> The men in the trenches lived under conditions of the deepest discomfort. For weeks together the communication trenches were knee-deep in water. Previous troops had dug deep sumpholes in the bottom of the trenches, covering them with boards, with the intention of draining off the water. But the water soon filled these and rose till it floated off the boards. Then would come some unfortunate fellow splashing his way along the trench, to plunge into the hole and be soused in icy water to the waist or higher. Men crawling their way through [the] mud experienced the sensations of flies in treacle.' [7]

But perhaps it was the 'war poets' who managed to describe the torment best. Siegfried Sassoon, in his poem *To the Warmongers* [8], wrote:

I'm back again from Hell
With loathsome thoughts to sell;
Secrets of death to tell;
And horrors from the abyss.
Young faces bleared with blood,
Sucked down into the mud,
You shall hear things like this,
Till the tormented slain
Crawl round and once again,
With limbs that twist awry
Moan out their brutish pain,
As the fighters pass them by.

And Wilfred Owen, in his poem *Anthem for Doomed Youth* [8], wrote:

What passing bells for those who die as cattle?
  Only the monstrous anger of the guns.
  Only the stuttering rifles' rapid rattle
Can patter out their hasty orisons.
No mockeries for them from prayers or bells,
  Nor any voice of mourning save the choirs,-
The shrill, demented choirs of wailing shells;
  And bugles calling for them from sad shires.

Sacrifice on the Somme

The Somme had been chosen for the offensive because the British and French armies could fight side by side, and originally there were to have been 40 French divisions and 25 British. In the event, the British fielded 14, but the French, as the tragedy of Verdun unfolded, had to limit their contribution to 5. Thus, for the first time, Great Britain was shouldering the main weight in a Western Front offensive.

The British C.-in-C., General Sir Douglas Haig, deliberately chose, as the point for the breakthrough, the strongest portion of the German line, believing that to be defeated there would most demoralise the Germans. The battle was opened by five days of intense bombardment on an eighteen-mile front. 1,738,000 shells were fired with the intention of destroying the enemy barbed wire and front line. Not only did it fail to do so, and Divisional commanders appear to have realised this but kept the knowledge to themselves, but it pitted the ground so heavily with shell craters orderly advance was made impossible.

Then, on the morning of 1st July 1916, a hundred thousand men left their trenches and moved forward at a steady walk. They had been drilled to advance in rigid parade-ground formation – straight lines two to three paces between each man, 100 yards between each rank in the assault waves. Even worse, they were all laden down with between 66 and 90 pounds of equipment: their own personal kit, which included water bottles, a day's rations, two gas masks, mess tins, spare socks, field dressings, rifle, bayonet, 220 rounds of ammunition, and an entrenching tool; some were also carrying hand grenades, mortar bombs, field telephones, or carrier pigeons. Indeed, the only advantage they possessed was their zeal and their courage. As they struggled across No Man's Land the German machine gunners emerged from their dug-outs and manned their guns. The carnage was about to begin. By the end of the day 20,000 British soldiers would be dead, and another 40,000 wounded or missing.

The 36th (Ulster) Division had been given the objective of capturing the German trenches beside the River Ancre, and north of the village of Thiepval. What made this task particularly difficult was that the battlefield was overlooked by the notorious Schwaben Redoubt, a formidable system of trenches and fortified machine gun posts.

The three Brigades of the 36th Division had the following objectives: north of the village of Hamel 108 Brigade was to attack astride the Ancre. From their positions at Thiepval Wood 109 Brigade was to take the south-east corner of the Schwaben Redoubt. Once they had achieved this, 107 Brigade was to follow them, then pass through the captured positions to storm the German fifth line. Brigadier R.J.C. Broadhurst has described the resulting battle:

> At first, south of the Ancre, everything went well, and 108 and 109 Brigades moved over the first German trenches with little loss. Scarcely were they across, however, when the German batteries opened a barrage on No Man's Land. Simultaneously the skilful and resolute German machine-gunners, who had remained safe from our bombardment, now sprang up from their shelters, pulling up their guns and heavy ammunition boxes, and raked our men from the flanks and the rear, thinning the khaki waves. Officers went down, and the men went on alone.
>
> Then a fearful misfortune struck them. Thiepval village on the right, a nest of German weapons, should have been taken by the 32nd Division. But the assaulting

troops had over-run it, and had been mown down from the rear by the German machine-gunners, likewise untouched by the bombardment. These guns now swung round and fired belt after belt of accurately aimed ammunition on the exposed Ulstermen. In dozens they fell dead or crawled wounded into the craters. Yet on the Inniskilling battalions pushed, the rear companies struggling over earth crimsoned with the deeds of their fallen comrades. With a wild Irish yell, they stormed the Schwaben Redoubt, quelling the doughty German machine-gunners who fired to the last. By 8.30 a.m., having covered a mile of devastated land in an hour of unremitting fighting, they had carried their objective.

On their left, 108 Brigade had advanced with equal ardour through equal tribulation. The 13th Irish Rifles, exposed to enfilade fire from the Beaucourt Redoubt across the River Ancre, lost nearly all its officers even before it reached the enemy trenches. The 11th Irish Rifles had its 'A' and 'D' Companies utterly obliterated – cut down like hay. But the supporting companies and the 15th Irish Rifles behind them pressed on over the dead and the dying. Great gaps began to appear in their lines. Never falling behind the rolling barrage, these troops, battalions in name only, assaulted and carried their objective, the north-east corner of the Schwaben Redoubt and the trenches running north.

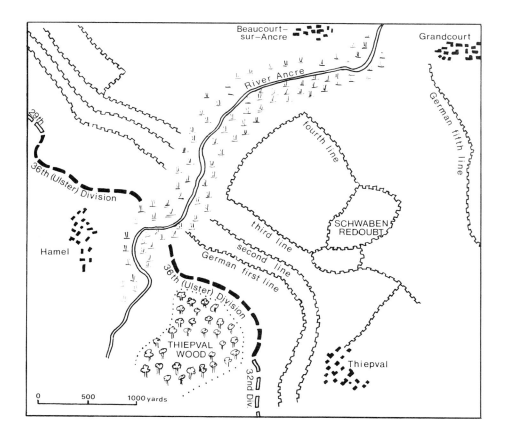

Their comrades across the Ancre, the 12th Irish Rifles and the 9th Royal Irish Fusiliers, with courage no less great, suffered immediate destruction. Held up by wire over the hill-brow undamaged by our bombardment, they fell behind our rolling barrage and were scourged by withering machine-gun fire. Twice the remnants were re-formed under their indomitable officers and again led forward and reduced to ruin.

Meanwhile, 107 Brigade, the 8th, 9th and 10th Irish Rifles, advancing through a tempest of fire, had passed, as planned, through 109 Brigade and occupied the German line before the Grandcourt line; their final objective 600 yards of open ground remained. Believing that all hazards must be dared for victory, the Rifles charged across. Two-thirds of them went down. The undaunted survivors leapt into the trenches, and seized them after desperate hand-to-hand fighting.' [6]

The Ulstermen had achieved a remarkable success, one that could have been turned to great tactical advantage. They had punched a vital salient into the German line – could it now be exploited? As Lt.-Colonel W. A. Shooter wrote: 'The Ulster Division, in spite of the fact that more than half its strength were now casualties, held in their grasp the promise of a great and far-reaching victory if the breach which they had made in the strongest part of the enemy defence system could have been put to use.' [9]

But nothing was done, and all the exhausted men in the captured trenches could do was wait for the inevitable German counter-attack, or listen to the sounds of their injured comrades. 'There was fellas crawlin' back that couldn't walk... One fella lay down, put down his rifle, covered himself with his groundsheet and when we came across him he was dead. No one to touch them! I used to think it was terrible to see young lives – the blood of life oozing out of them. Nobody there to lift their head – not one – nobody there to care – that was it!' [10]

E. A. Mackintosh expressed similar feelings:[8]

Oh, never will I forget you,	Happy and young and gallant,
My men that trusted me,	They saw their first-born go,
More my sons than your fathers',	But not the strong limbs broken
For they could only see	And the beautiful men brought low,
The little helpless babies	The piteous writhing bodies,
And the young men in their pride.	They screamed 'Don't leave me, sir,'
They could not see you dying,	For they were only your fathers
And hold you while you died.	But I was your officer.

At dusk on 1 July a powerful counter-attack by fresh German troops drove the Ulstermen, almost weaponless, back to the second German line, which they held all next day, tattered and exhausted, until relieved at night by the 49th Division. Four VCs and many other decorations were to be awarded to them for their bravery. 'They had lost over five thousand five hundred officers and men. The Inniskillings lost more than any British regiment of the line has ever lost in a single day. Of the 15th Royal Irish Rifles, only 70 men answered their names that night of the 1st of July.' [6] The dead accounted for half of these casualties.

A ration party of the 12th Royal Irish Rifles

Comrades in Arms

Irish troops had already been well blooded in the war. They had fought gallantly at Sedd-el-Bahr and Suvla Bay, during the ill-fated landings in the Dardanelles. Of that particular episode Brigadier-General W.B. Marshal had written: 'Though I am an Englishman, I must say the Irish soldiers have fought magnificently. They are the cream of the Army. Ireland may well be proud of her sons. Ireland has done her duty nobly. Irishmen are absolutely indispensable for our final triumph.' And Captain Thornhill, of the New Zealand Force said: 'Your Irish soldiers are the talk of the whole Army. Their landing at Suvla Bay was the greatest thing that you will ever read of in books. Those who witnessed the advance will never forget it.' [2]

In the Battle of the Somme, as well as the sacrifice made by the men of the 36th (Ulster) Division, battalions of Irishmen and Ulstermen fought elsewhere along the battle front, particularly in the 16th (Irish) Division. This Division included five Ulster battalions and also the 6th Battalion The Connaught Rangers, which contained over 600 Ulstermen recruited mainly from West Belfast.

During the battle the 16th (Irish) Division is most prominently identified with the assaults on the villages of Guillemont and Ginchy in September. As Lt.-Colonel W.A. Shooter described it:

> The conditions in which the Irishmen had to advance were appalling. The whole of this area was a scene of complete desolation and odious mud, churned up by continuous British bombardment during many unsuccessful attacks on this stubborn bastion since the Battle of the Somme opened on 1st July. Movement over the ground in such conditions required a supreme effort, apart altogether from the fierce hurricane of machine-gun and artillery fire which the enemy brought to bear on the advancing troops. Nevertheless, the advancing Fusiliers and Riflemen hacked their way forward with great determination and traditional Irish dash, in spite of the most severe casualties and drove the Germans from their positions, inflicting heavy loss on the defenders and taking many prisoners. A fierce enemy counter-attack on the newly-won position in Leuze Wood was decisively beaten off by the two Inniskilling Battalions and the whole of the line firmly held. The newly-won ground had to be defended stubbornly for the next few days against many hostile onslaughts. The enemy realised he had lost an important key position and put in great efforts to regain the position lost to the Irishmen.
>
> On September 9th the 16th Division again greatly distinguished itself by capturing the closely neighbouring village of Ginchy in an equally brilliant fashion. The Ulstermen of the Inniskillings, the Irish Fusiliers and the Rifles, advanced with great determination through a fierce barrage of enemy fire so intense as to suggest that not even an insect could have survived in that hail of fire and death.' [9]

When this new line had been consolidated a renewed assault was made on 15th September, during which 'tanks' made their first appearance on a battlefield. The Guards Division which launched itself forward from their positions at Ginchy included two battalions of the Irish Guards, the 1st and 2nd. The Germans, aided by the fact that the assault by the 6th Division between Ginchy and Leuze Wood had failed, mainly due to the driving fire from the strongly fortified redoubt known as the 'Quadrilateral', were able to give the Guards

Division their complete attention. Every shell-burst and burst of machine-gun fire found its way among their ranks, but they pressed forward and managed to hold on to the ground they had gained.

Both of the Irish Guards battalions had suffered heavily – one hundred and sixty-six survivors were all that remained of the 2nd Battalion when the roll was called.

On the 25th September a new attack was opened. The British artillery fire was much better than on the 15th and it enabled the Guards Division to take all their objectives one after the other until finally they had fought through to the northern end of Les Boeufs where they consolidated and firmly held the position. But there had been a high price to pay for this victory - in the two attacks on the 15th and 25th the 1st Battalion of the Irish Guards had lost 99% of its strength.

> General Rawlinson, who commanded the IVth Army, said it was the vigorous attacks of the Guards Division under very trying conditions which won the day. They pressed forward the attack in face of a great concentration of enfilade fire from both flanks. Perhaps it would be right to say that the Guards Division by their success in capturing these key enemy positions was one of the main reasons which forced the eventual German withdrawal 'according to plan' to the Hindenburg Line. [9]

Men of the 16th (Irish) Division returning after the capture of Guillemont

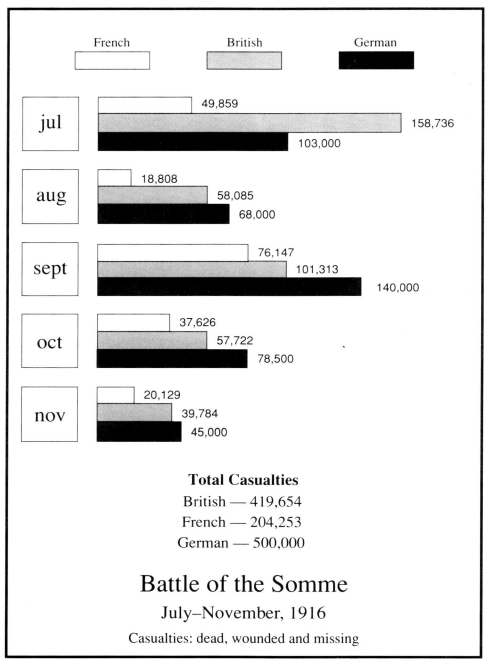

French **British** **German**

	French	British	German
jul	49,859	158,736	103,000
aug	18,808	58,085	68,000
sept	76,147	101,313	140,000
oct	37,626	57,722	78,500
nov	20,129	39,784	45,000

Total Casualties

British — 419,654

French — 204,253

German — 500,000

Battle of the Somme

July–November, 1916

Casualties: dead, wounded and missing

Source: Purnell's History of the 20th Century

Side by Side

After the Battle of the Somme the 36th (Ulster) Division was withdrawn to make good its terrible losses, and transferred to Flanders. On 7 June 1917 it took part in the Battle of Messines. This was the first completely successful single operation on the British front. But there was another important ingredient to it. As H.E.D. Harris pointed out: 'It is also memorable to Irishmen as largely an all-Irish achievement; two of the three divisions in the attacking line were Irish, the 36th on the right and the 16th in the centre of IX Corps, a unique line-up of Irish fighting men, and the largest in modern history.' [11]

The Messines-Wytschaete Ridge was a narrow feature which dominated the surrounding landscape, giving the Germans a perfect view of the British lines. Unless the ridge could be taken no break-out from the Ypres Salient would be possible. The preparations for the attack were extensive and thorough. A concerted attempt was made to leave no aspect overlooked. An elaborate model of the ridge, with trenches, forts, roads and woods, was constructed, surrounded by a wooden gallery and trench-board walks, so that at least a company could examine it at one time.

Attacks were practised over ground marked out to represent the enemy trench system. The provision of food, water, ammunition, and stores for the advancing troops was planned and prepared – at an early stage in the assault the troops were even served with hot tea! Means of communication – by visual signalling, pigeons, wireless, fullerphone, runners, and rockets for S.O.S. calls – were worked out in detail.

Cyril Falls described other preparations:

> Each morning air photographs, showing the effect of the previous day's bombardment, were circulated to Divisions in the line. Each Division was required to state, day by day, what further special bombardment it desired. From its observation post on Kemmel Hill the Staff of the 36th Division could see practically all the slope of the Messines ridge. Day by day it studied the ground during the bombardment. A trench or concrete work which did not appear to have been sufficiently shelled was noted, and request made that it should receive further attention next day. Such requests were invariably met. Trenches and dug-outs were shelled again and again, till Divisional Headquarters declared itself satisfied' [7]

As well as this a series of mines were to be detonated under the German positions – the greatest ever mining operation in land warfare. German geology professors said the water-logged ground would not permit tunnelling, but nine companies of tunnellers toiling for a year were to prove otherwise. On the day of the attack 'the great semi-circle of mines exploded, spewing up, as it seemed, the solid earth, of which fragments fell half a mile away, and sending to the skies great towers of crimson flame, that hung a moment ere they were choked by the clouds of dense black smoke which followed them from their caverns. There came first one ghastly flash of light, then a shuddering of earth thus outraged, then the thunder-clap. General Nugent, returning to his command post on Kemmel from the observation post a hundred yards away, declared that the sight he had seen was a "vision of hell".' [7]

The boundary line between the 36th (Ulster) Division and the 16th (Irish) Division ran along the main street of Wytschaete, half the village being in the objective of each

Division. When the attack ended all the objectives had been taken. Casualties among the Irish troops were comparatively light for a Western Front battle. In the 36th Division, 61 officers and 1,058 other ranks; in the 16th, under 1,000, all ranks. One of the casualties of the 16th Division was Major William Redmond, MP, brother of John Redmond. Because of his age (fifty-seven) he wasn't required to go 'over the top', and had been attached for duty to Divisional Headquarters, but he had insisted on accompanying his men. He was brought in by stretcher bearers of the Ulster Division, but although his wound was light, he wasn't young or fit enough to stand the strain and shock and died a few hours later.

Harris commented:

> They showed to the world the sight of nearly 30,000 Irishmen shoulder to shoulder, men of all four provinces, and the only rivalry that existed between them was that of gallantry. In his book *As from Kemmel Hill*, Andrew Behrend wrote: "I should like to put on record one further memory of the Battle of Messines. However little it interested me then, it fascinates me today; that during this battle and for weeks before, the 16th (Irish) and the 36th (Ulster) Divisions lived and fought side by side, got on with each other splendidly and at times even pulled each other's chestnuts out of the fire ...".[11]

The two Irish Divisions next took part in the series of battles known as Third Ypres, which began on 31 July and went on continuously until 10 November 1917, costing 244,897 British casualties and about 337,000 German.

On 16 August there was an offensive attack on Langemarck, the two divisions selected to lead the attack being the 16th (Irish) and the 36th (Ulster). Battalions of the Royal Irish Fusiliers linked the two Divisions. The men of the 7th and 8th were on the left of the 16th

The Third Battle of Ypres – men of the 36th (Ulster) Division, 1917

Division, and those of the 9th on the extreme right of the 36th Division, so these battalions advanced side by side. 'The ground was a swamp, the weather was atrocious, and through a morass of shell-holes, in which wounded men were drowned, the attack was pressed home; but in the process various units, notably the 9th Battalion Royal Irish Fusiliers, were all but annihilated. This long and desperate fight was like a nightmare. In some respects, says Col. Buchan, the histories have no parallel for colossal difficulty and naked misery among the shell-holes and tortured ridges of the Ypres salient. It was a soldiers' battle, and as such was made conspicuous by gallant deeds.'[12]

When the Germans counter-attacked the 9th Royal Irish Fusiliers tried to dig in on Hill 35 but with their C.O. and many others killed there were too few to withstand the assault. As Philip Gibbs wrote: 'The counter-attacks drove in the thinned but still determined line of Irishmen, and they came back across the riddled ground, some of them wounded, all in the last stages of exhaustion, pausing in their unwilling journey to fire at snipers who harassed them, and reaching at last the trenches they left at dawn, angry and bitter and disappointed, but undismayed – the heroes of a splendid failure.'[12]

The last phase in the Third Battle of Ypres, from 4 October to 6 November was fought for the almost obliterated village of Passchendaele. Rain fell almost unceasingly throughout October, and Passchendaele became known to history as the 'battle of the mud'. Instead of the hoped-for break-through to clear the Flanders coast, it turned into a terrible battle of attrition, where men and animals alike drowned in the quagmire. General Gough wrote:

> The guns churned this treacherous slime. Every day conditions grew worse. What had once been difficult now became impossible. The surplus water poured into the trenches as its natural outlet, and they became impassable for troops; nor was it possible to walk over the open field – men staggered warily over duckboard tracks. Wounded men falling headlong into the shell-holes were in danger of drowning. Mules slipped from the tracks and were often drowned in the giant shell-holes alongside. Guns sank till they became useless; rifles caked and would not fire; even food was tainted with the inevitable mud. No battle in history was ever fought under such conditions as that of Passchendaele.

On 20 November 1917 the 16th and 36th Divisions took part in the Battle of Cambrai, when 380 tanks were used in the assault. The 16th Division attacked on a three-brigade front, and were immediately successful. At zero hour the leading troops went 'over the top' and were across No-man's-land into the famous Tunnel Trench within moments of the barrage lifting. However, when the enemy counter-attacks were launched there was desperate hand-to-hand fighting for several hours.

On the main sector the most difficult task fell to the 36th Division. They were to attack the Hindenburg Line on the Canal du Nord, a wide canal with deep sides. After close and fierce fighting 109th Brigade broke through and stormed the mound. 'The divisional staff had foreseen the difficulty of crossing the dry canal and prepared for it. Ex-Belfast shipwrights serving in the Divisional Engineers threw a temporary bridge over the ravine and the infantry charged across it. By 16:00 hours the Cambrai-Bapaume road was crossed and the main Hindenburg Line entered - an advance of 4,000 yards.'[11]

On 21 March 1918 the Germans launched a massive attack against the Allied positions. After a terrific bombardment, massed German divisions surged forward at 09:40 hours.

The 16th (Irish) Division was to receive a terrible battering. Two companies of the 7th Royal Irish Regiment posted in the Forward Zone were smothered completely; not one man managed to escape. Attacking the village of Ronnsoy, held by the 7th and 8th Royal Inniskilling Fusiliers, the Germans, after a fierce struggle, managed to occupy the village by noon, although some posts held out until evening. But by then all the men of the Inniskillings had been killed or captured. The garrison of Lempire, the 2nd Royal Irish Regiment, came under attack on three sides, and after a desperate resistance most of this battalion were killed or captured. The British Official History says: 'Three-quarters of the Fifth Army battalions in the Forward Zone ceased to exist as units, whilst in the rest only a few officers and men remained. The losses were severest in 14 and 16 Divisions leaving them with little further fighting strength. The 16th Division continued by strenuous efforts to delay the enemy's advance whilst guns were got away.'

In the south the Germans had made faster progress. Here the 36th (Ulster) Division was part of the British XVIII Corps. The German attack was so swift and concentrated that few of the out-post troops managed to get back to the line of resistance. The 12th Royal Irish Rifles held out until 15:15 hours. The 15th Royal Irish Rifles and 2nd Inniskillings held out against repeated attacks until after 18:00 hours. But eventually they were all overwhelmed.

The next day the British divisions began ordered withdrawals. But one position, the Ricardo Redoubt, occupied by the 1st Inniskillings, was surrounded and cut off. 'Here Colonel Crawford's men fought doggedly on. In the afternoon he sent away a party which managed to get back to our lines but the remainder fought on until, driven by bombers and pounded by trench mortars into a corner of the Redoubt, "a mere handful was taken prisoner at 6 p.m." ' [11] As Brigadier A.E.C. Bredin commented, the 16th and 36th Divisions 'suffered the heaviest losses of any formation during the great German offensive of March, 1918.' [13]

But after these initial German successes their offensive faltered. They may not have realised it then, but it was to have been their last real chance to turn the war in their favour. The Allies armies had been battered, but not defeated. Put under a united command at last, the Allies began to launch their counter-attacks. The Germans still had plenty of fighting potential, but behind them their own allies began to collapse, through war weariness, privation and military defeat. All the German army could hope for now was a fighting retreat. Indeed, when the Armistice was finally signed, the German army, still unbroken, stood everywhere on foreign soil, except for a few villages which the French had held throughout the war in Alsace.

The Devastation in France

■ 1,500 schools destroyed

■ 1,200 churches destroyed

■ 377 public buildings destroyed

■ 1,000 industrial plants destroyed

■ 246,000 other buildings destroyed

■ 1,875 sq. miles of forest laid waste

■ 8,000 sq. miles of agricultural land laid waste

The record of the Thirty-sixth Division will ever be the pride of Ulster. At Thiepval in the great battle of the Somme on July 1st, 1916; at Wytschaete on June 17th, 1917, in the storming of the Messines Ridge; on the Canal du Nord, in the attack on the Hindenburg Line of November 20th in the same year; on March 21, 1918, near Fontaine-les-Clercs, defending their positions long after they were isolated and surrounded by the enemy; and later in the month at Andechy in the days of 'backs to the wall', they acquired a reputation for conduct and devotion deathless in the military history of the United Kingdom, and repeatedly signalised in the despatches of the Commander-in-Chief.

Winston Churchill

North of Thiepval the Ulster Division broke through the enemy trenches, passed the crest of the ridge, and reached the point called The Crucifix, in rear of the first German position. For a little while they held the strong Schwaben Redoubt (where), enfiladed on three sides, they went on through successive German lines, and only a remnant came back to tell the tale. Nothing finer was done in the war. The splendid troops drawn from those Volunteers who had banded themselves together for another cause now shed their blood like water for the liberty of the world.

Colonel John Buchan, *History of the War*

I am not an Ulsterman, but yesterday, the 1st July, as I followed their amazing attack, I felt that I would rather be an Ulsterman than anything else in the world. My pen cannot describe adequately the hundreds of heroic acts that I witnessed... The Ulster Volunteer Force, from which the Division was made, has won a name which equals any in history. Their devotion deserves the gratitude of the British Empire.

Captain W. B. Spender

It is these soldiers of ours, with their astonishing courage and their beautiful faith, with their natural military genius, with their tenderness as well as strength; carrying with them their green flags and their Irish war-pipes; advancing to the charge, their fearless officers at their head, and followed by their beloved chaplains as great-hearted as themselves; bringing with them a quality all their own to the sordid modern battlefield; exhibiting the character of the Irishman at its noblest and greatest. May Ireland, cherishing them in her bosom, know how to prove her love and pride and send their brothers leaping to keep full their battle-torn ranks and to keep high and glad their heroic hearts!

John Redmond

Our greatest success (on the 3rd September 1916) was the capture of Guillemont by the Irish troops. They advanced on Guillemont with an impetuosity which carried all before it: charged through the German positions with the wild music of their pipes playing them on. Before the afternoon was out the 2000 Prussians who constituted the garrison - with imperative orders to hold the ground at all cost - were killed, wounded, or captured. The same Irish troops charged into Ginchy as they had charged into Guillemont, through the barrage of shells and the storm of machine-gun fire, clambering over shell-holes, fallen trees, and the great mounds of bricks and rubble which were all that remained of the village itself; cheering like mad, and driving the enemy before them in a fierce assault against which nothing could stand.

Frank A. Mumby, *The Great World War - A History*

Undiminished Memories

Jack Christie, born 10 February 1898

I left school at about twelve years of age and went to serve my time in the old Ulster Spinning Company, in the Falls Road branch. I hated it, for I had to start at six and it was a dreadful time to get up at. My mother used to get up to make my breakfast and get me out, and I can still get the feeling now of how she looked at me going out in the cold and dark to make my way to the mill. We got three-quarters of an hour for our dinner and I had to run home from the Falls Road to the Shankill, and then rush back again. I hated it.

So when I came to join up when the War came, it wasn't a challenge or anything to do with patriotism, it was simply: here's an escape route to get out of the mill, for surely life holds more than what this mill can offer?

I had become a first aid man in the U.V.F. and I remember marching down the Shankill Road in a body to the Old Town Hall and joining up there. For a while there was no place to put us, but it was great – no work to do, free travel – as far as I remember – on the trams, and more important we got into the Falls baths free; we were great swimmers my wee crowd. The great thing about the 36th Division was that they were all comrades, they were all from the one place. We didn't know everybody, but we knew they were Ulster people, and we'd the people that we went to school with in our lot; we were a very young lot.

Yet the comradeship that came out of it, was something that had to grow; it didn't come to fruition till we went to France. And you weren't aware of it, it was just something that... Look, if you want to know about comradeship, would you believe me that after the 1st of July, after the battle, after all the horror, when I went home on leave I found that I was missing my comrades. The funny thing in a way, was that your old friends, your old pals that you knew before the war, who hadn't joined up, didn't want you. And I just wanted to be back with my boys again, with my comrades.

There's all this emphasis on the Somme, and while it was unique because of the slaughter, I still had some happy times there. I was in Thiepval Wood for maybe a couple of months preparing for the 1st July, and although they were throwing shells over at us, and the work was hard, somehow it still didn't detract from the enjoyment of the nights being with your mates in the dug-outs.

But a place like Ypres was never like that. Ypres was hell from beginning to end. It was an unbelievable flipping place – it should have had 'Abandon Hope' written up all over it. I had a dreadful experience at Passchendaele. I remember a fellow from Dublin, one of our fellows – we got a contingent from Dublin one time – and he said to me, just out of the blue: 'Jack, if I get out of here I'll be a changed man.'

I think it's admitted by all sides that the Ulster Division was a really good division. The reputation they had is such an honourable one it doesn't need anyone to say anything to add to it, or to try to fit it into one tradition. Do you know what I'm trying to say? We should never let politics blind us to the truth about things – bravery and loyalty wasn't all on one side. The 16th Division played a vital part alongside of us. We'd always the greatest respect for them – except for the odd hardliner that's always there – we'd great regard for the 16th. The 16th were with us at Messines. I remember there were four of us in this advance post dealing with the wounded of the 19th Royal Irish Rifles. And just over the brow of the hill some of the 16th had their wee dug-out, and we went across, a couple of us at a time, to have a yarn with them, and they came across too, a couple at a time, always leaving a couple at the first aid post -- and we became great friends.

We had a football team and I unfortunately had to keep the ball all the time, although it wasn't easy to carry it about with you. Our sleeping quarters were everywhere and any wee corner you could get into. We got this old barn one time and I was sleeping in the hay-loft and the other men were all down below. And here didn't the rats scrape and scrape and scrape and nearly drive me up the walls. I had to get up in the middle of the night, and I threw the ball down at them, and it bounced from one man to another, and they called me for everything for throwing it down. But the blinking rats were driving me up the walls, they were terrible!

Before the Battle of the Somme started I captured a German; well, I didn't capture him as much as he came up to me with his hands up. And some of the men – like, all you could see was the tops of their heads looking up over the trench – well, anyway, they were shouting at me: 'Shoot him , Tommy, shoot him!' But I didn't like to shoot the man in cold blood, it wouldn't have been right anyway. So I took him down a hill and searched him at the bottom, but he had nothing on him – we got word at one time that the Germans had been using daggers. I don't believe it though, because I don't think the Germans were really bad people or wicked in any way, as far as I could see. So I walked him along to where the reserves were coming up and I told him to go on down there, and he walked down the hill with his hands up, and that was the last I saw of him.

I went back to my own battalion as the attack had opened up, and I went in with them. I didn't get very far until somebody fired a gun and hit me in the leg. I fired back at him and hit him in the face, and I could see the blood shooting out of his face, in gushes like, coming out of his cheek. He was a nice looking young man but he was a sniper, and if I hadn't got him God knows how many people he would have killed before we would have got him.

Anyway I was still able to walk and I went down into the trench. I only got a few yards when a shell burst above my head and I was all shrapnel in my shoulders and my back; my arms had pieces of shrapnel everywhere, so I went out for the count right there. When I wakened up again on the 4th of July I was in Colchester Hospital. I don't remember how I got from France to England. When I wakened up I saw two nurses standing looking at me and they laughed and one of them says 'there's a wee souvenir for you' – it was two wee bags made out of pieces of lint and they were filled with wee pieces of shrapnel and a bullet that was taken out of me.

I remember we were running up the trenches, and on the way here's this fellow lying at his machine gun, tired looking. As I looked at this gunner I recognised him. I used to carry the goods home for my mother at the weekends, and Mr. O'Hagan, who owned the grocer's shop where my mother dealt in, had this display, a biscuit cabinet. And Mr. O'Hagan used to say to this bloke 'Austin, tidy up those broken biscuits please.' So when I was running past him I shouted 'Austin, tidy up those broken biscuits please.' He shouted: 'Who said that, who said that!' We had to move on, but it was rather funny, with everybody asking me what the hell it was I said to him. When I met him going to work years later, he says: 'do you know I thought I was going crackers then.'

I remember too we were in a village close to the men of the 16th Irish Division, and a lot of Australians. This Australian, a great fella, but very overbearing... anyway, something happened and there was a row between some of our people and these Australians. How the Irish Brigade got word of it nobody knew, but down they came and beat up the Australians. Now I saw fellas, I saw fellas arm in arm afterwards, fellas of the 11th Inniskillings with their orange and purple patches, and the other fellas with the big green patch on their arm...

John Spencer tells this story: There was a halt in the marching, and he was hanging over this gateway when down comes a nun. John says 'Bonjour Mademoiselle', and she replies 'what are you blithering about?' I think she said she was from Kilkenny, but what on earth she was doing there we couldn't imagine. She was a lovely girl and John talked about it with great gusto, oh yes, it was his pet story.

There were lots of funny things as well as terrible things. Yes, some things do distress me. Now when you first came to interview me, things kept poppin' up on me, I couldn't sleep for weeks, things just came back. People ask me how I can remember the names of all those villages, but I can't forget it. I belong to the Methodist Church, the little church in Ballynafeigh. I lay the wreath there on Armistice day. I think there were eighteen names on that hall table there; I knew them everyone, and when it comes up it bothers me. I just hate that time of year, it brings things up.

24

Jack Campbell, born 26 September, 1895

I was born at 12, Eugene Street, in Dublin. There was five of us – brothers, no sisters. The eldest brother was always on about seeing the world. Well, we weren't financially in a position to go and see the world. He figured out that by joining the Army you could see the world – you could see the next bloody world too, but there you are! So he went, and of course we all went. The eldest brother was a Battery Sergeant Major in the Royal Canadian Horse Artillery. Next one to him, Pat, he was killed at Vimy Ridge. The next was in the Royal Dublin Fusiliers. He was killed at Maricourt on the Somme. The day he was killed I got gassed.

I joined up in Dublin in 1912, in my mother's maiden name, Larkin, because I wasn't of age and my parents could've claimed me out. The recruiting sergeant in Dublin told me I could do that. I joined the Royal Army Medical Corps attached to the Black Watch...

We were all the same then, all went to school together and played games together. In them days there was no such thing as caring what your religion was. We had a bunch of four or five Protestants in our school gang. We got on very well together, respected each other, grew up together, enjoyed each other's company. There was no such thing as 'you were a Protestant, and I was a Catholic' – that's a silly business altogether. I respect everybody's religion...

I'll tell you how I got gassed. We were out on a working party this day on the Somme. And I think Jerry must have spotted us, for he sent over a barrage. And during this barrage we jumped for shell-holes or wherever you could get a bit of cover. And I got hit on the hip; there was no gas around, but I had my gas mask over my left shoulder. And I got hit on my left hip, and well, it was a pretty hard bang I got, it knocked me several feet into a shell-hole.

Course right away I looked at myself to see if I was wounded. But I wasn't wounded and I passed no remarks, see, and carried on during the day. And that night an officer came along and said there was some wounded out in front of the trench. There was about ten of us went out for to get them in, and while we were out Jerry must have seen us, because he sent gas over, and of course we had to get the masks on.

Well, I put my mask on and, well I hadn't it on a couple of minutes when I began to feel sick. I had to pull it off or I would've got sick into it, you see, then I staggered around for a bit and then I went down. 'Cause me eyes they were paining me and everything like that, and a fella came along and said, 'where're you hit , mate?' So I said, 'I'm gassed.' So when he bent down he said 'no wonder you're gassed mate, there's a piece of German shell in the metal container of your gas mask.' That was what hit me during the day and I never noticed it...

Look, the 'Old Contemptibles' were a different type altogether. We had a very deep friendship for each other. You know there's only thirty-three of us left out of that British Army that went overseas in 1914. I'm the only one left in Ireland, I'm the last 'Old Contemptible' in Ireland. I belong to the Royal British Legion, and we tried through the British Legion in Ireland to find out if there's any 'Old Contemptible' here – and there isn't. I'm the last one in Ireland. The others are all scattered around Britain, but we're all meeting in July in London. The 'Old Contemptibles' had a sense of sharing. We shared our last cigarette, we shared our last bite of food, we shared our lives actually, because we risked our lives to help each other.

The Irish were there in great numbers – look at the VCs the Irish won, and all that kind of thing. The 36th Division was a wonderful division, they really won their laurels, they did; their casualties were terrific. Everyone knew that about them. I heard about them, the cutting-up they got, when I was on the Somme. The Irish, they really made a name for themselves.

At that time the local population here in Ballyclare was about two and a half thousand, and out of that total over four hundred and fifty people turned up to enlist, men and women – the women joined as nurses of course.

Well, when we first went out of course the trenches were in an awful state; they just had them cut, and they were in a rough way. There were no duck boards or foot boards down, and there was no drainage. The result was that you were going along up to your knees in mud. The winter of 1915 was terrible because we weren't prepared for it, but later on they issued us with either waders or big heavy leather boots that came up to your knee, which was more helpful.

The sleeping quarters were rough, very rough sometimes, and the whole front was infested with rats – they were there by the million, terrific big brutes they were too. The rats were so bad we had to hang what kind of beds we were able to make from the ceiling, to get clear of the rats down below. They were wild altogether, and your food... Two of you joined together with your food rations – the food was put in the hollow of one steel helmet and the second helmet clamped over the top, and then the two wired round so the rats couldn't get at it. Then of course when you were in the dug-outs up forward you were just like the rats, crawling about on your hands and knees...

On the 1st of July we had to attack a great fortification that the Germans had built, the Schwaben Redoubt, and they said that it couldn't be taken, and they were quite definite about that there. And our own army commanders were of the same opinion, but it had to be attacked; and the most peculiar thing of the whole Somme battle that day was that the Ulster Division was the only one that reached their objective out of all the divisions.

I remember reading where a French correspondent was sending a dispatch to his newspaper about the Ulster attack, and I think he described it very well indeed. He said that the youth of Ulster entered the Battle of the Somme as enthusiastic young sportsmen and emerged from it as professional soldiers. I think he summed it up well. In Ballyclare alone that day, out of the small community we had there, there were over thirty men killed and over one hundred wounded. You know, that was an awful, an awful total for such a small community. And I'm the only Somme veteran left in Ballyclare.

I went back to the Somme on the 60th anniversary. To be quite frank it was an emotional return. The whole place was quite different from when we were there before. Then it was all trenches, barbed wire and shell-holes, but when we went back it was the most beautiful place you could have been to. And that day, when I was signing the visitor's book at the Ulster Tower I remembered that I had also signed the book in Helen's Tower at Clandeboye camp. So my name is in both towers.

Many pens have tried to depict the ghastly expanse of mud which covered this waterlogged country, but few have been able to paint a picture sufficiently intense. Imagine a fertile countryside, dotted every few hundred yards with peasant farms and an occasional hamlet; water everywhere, for only an intricate system of small drainage canals relieved the land from the ever-present danger of flooding... Then imagine this same countryside battered, beaten, and torn by a torrent of shell and explosive... such as no land in the world had yet witnessed – the soil shaken and reshaken, fields tossed into new and fantastic shapes, roads blotted out from the landscape, houses and hamlets pounded into dust so thoroughly that no man could point to where they stood, and the intensive and essential drainage system utterly and irretrievably destroyed. This alone presents a battle-ground of tremendous difficulty. But then came the incessant rain. The broken earth became a fluid clay; the little brooks and tiny canals became formidable obstacles, and every shell-hole a dismal pond; hills and valleys alike were but waves and troughs of a gigantic sea of mud.
General Gough, Commander Fifth Army

The Human Cost of the Great War

USA – 114,095

British Empire – 251,900

Turkey – 375,000

Italy – 460,000

Great Britain – 761,213

Austria-Hungary – 1,100,000

France – 1,358,000

Russia – 1,700,000

Germany – 2,000,000

Deaths at sea and in air raids – 100,000

Civilian loss of life

Belgium – 30,000

Rumania – 800,000

Germany – 812,296

Serbia and Austria – 1,000,000

Russia – 2,000,000

Massacre of Armenians, Jews, Syrians & Greeks – 4,000,000

Deaths due to famine, disease and starvation except where otherwise stated

Source: Purnell's History of the 20th Century

Homecoming

When the men of the 36th (Ulster) Division went 'over the top' on 1 July, 1916, news of the sacrifice they had made took some days filtering back to the community in Ulster. Then began a grief that was both private and communal at the same time, for in a community as closely-knit as the one existing in the north of Ireland, especially in Belfast, there could be no such thing as a purely individual loss, family networks and community feeling making sure of that. 'In the long streets of Belfast mothers looked out in dread for the red bicycles of the telegram boys. In house after house blinds were drawn down, until it seemed that every family in the city had been bereaved.' [14]

Gradually the full extent of the carnage became understood. At noon on 12 July the traffic of Belfast came to a halt, and in the pouring rain the citizens of the town stood in silence to remember the dead. The usual 'Twelfth' celebrations were cancelled, and all work was suspended.

Yet while Irishmen of all persuasions were dying side by side in the mud of France, the Irish conflict itself had not gone away. Even a World War wasn't enough to interfere with Irish history, for a few months before the sacrifice on the Somme, another blood sacrifice had been made much closer to hand – in Dublin.

A group of Irish Nationalists had felt that the promise of Home Rule wasn't enough – nothing short of an Irish Republic was acceptable – and a Rising in Dublin was planned for Easter 1916. But a Rising against England was the last thing Dublin was expecting. Thousands of Irish families had fathers, sons, brothers and husbands fighting in the trenches, and when the first Irishmen to win the V.C. in the war returned home in 1915 they had been given a tumultuous reception.

Even among those who were to lead the rising there were uncertainties as to the path they were embarking upon. James Connolly, just as he had previously declared that the World War was not for the benefit of the working classes of Europe, now wondered whether the Irish working class should spill their blood for a middle-class revolution that would leave them no better off than before. The leaders of the conspiracy met with him to try and convince him to give his support. After what he himself called a 'terrible mental struggle' he finally became fired with enthusiasm, sending a message to his wife, 'I have been beaten on my own ground.'[3] Yet he warned his followers: 'In the event of victory, hold on to your rifles, as those with whom we are fighting may stop before our goal is reached. We are out for economic as well as political liberty.'

When the Rising did take place the citizens of Dublin were far from sympathetic. The Volunteers who had taken over Jacob's Biscuit Factory 'were jeered by a hostile crowd... telling them if they wanted to fight, they should go out and fight in France.' [15] Indeed, while the leaders of the Rising hoped that their own sacrifice, no matter how elitist, would be seen as having been made for the sake of the Irish people, the only immediate benefit was the excuse it gave the poor of Dublin to go out on a widespread looting spree. When the Rising was finally defeated 60 rebels, 130 British soldiers and 300 civilians lay dead.

But it was the British government themselves who set the seal on events. Over a period of ten days fifteen leaders of the Rising were executed, and Irish opinion was finally swayed in favour of their rebellious fellow citizens, however misguided they might have seemed at the time – the 'blood sacrifice' had been made complete.

So when the war ended in Europe the soldiers returned to an Ireland where divisions were growing more intractable every day. Seventy-three Sinn Féin MPs were elected in 1918, but rather than sit at Westminster they set up their own assembly in Dublin, Dáil Eireann. On 21 January 1919 they proclaimed the Irish Republic, and when Dáil Eireann was declared illegal by the British government, guerrilla warfare by the I.R.A. was begun against the British security forces.

On 6 December 1921 the Anglo-Irish Treaty was signed in London. It gave twenty-six counties of Ireland Dominion status, and the 'Irish Free State' was born. Six northern counties, however, were allowed to opt out. Many were unhappy at this state of affairs and some of those who wished for a fully independent Irish Republic were to take up arms against the new Free State government. In the North, nationalists resented this 'partition' of the island, while Protestants were fearful that the newly-established Boundary Commission was going to whittle away their new Northern Ireland. Both communities in Ulster felt themselves beleaguered. Suspicion, fear, and intolerance increased. By the end of 1922 over 450 people would have become victims of the violence that inevitably resulted.

So only a few years after the end of the European war, the people of Ulster became engaged in a fratricidal conflict that would consume their energies so negatively and so repeatedly over the decades ahead. The tragedy overseas on the Somme was now to be overtaken by an even deeper tragedy at home, a tragedy that is still being visited upon the great grandchildren of the men who fought in the mud of France.

The General Post Office, Dublin, after the Easter Rising, 1916

29

Shock Waves

A. J. P. Taylor wrote: 'The Somme set the picture by which future generations saw the First World War: brave helpless soldiers; blundering obstinate generals; nothing achieved. After the Somme men decided that the war would go on for ever. Idealism perished on the Somme. The enthusiastic volunteers were enthusiastic no longer. They had lost faith in their cause, in their leaders, in everything except loyalty to their fighting comrades. The war ceased to have a purpose. It went on for its own sake, as a contest in endurance.' [4]

In retrospect 1916 proved to be the watershed of the First World War. Yet it was more than that – it marked the beginning of the end for the pre-War Europe. When the war finally ceased the old order in Europe was fundamentally changed, with Empires dissolved, new nations in existence and a fever of nationalism and revolution on the ascendant.

On the Eastern Front the terrible human cost of the war was to lend its own impetus to the revolutionary fervour that would finally sweep away the last of the Tsars, and usher in the new Soviet Russia.

On the Western Front too a crisis rapidly developed. When General Nivelle replaced Joffre in command of the French armies, he planned an ambitious offensive. A million men were to take part in the main assault, to be launched on 16 April 1917. It turned out to be an unmitigated disaster and ground to a halt in a fortnight. Instead of the great breakthrough envisaged, the troops only gained a few miles of ground at the price of almost 200,000 casualties.

But this time the 'unknown soldier' was taking no more. In bitter frustration and resentment the French army rebelled. For six weeks elements of fifty-four divisions, including a crack infantry regiment which had been in constant action since fighting gallantly at Verdun, refused to obey orders, called for peace, brandished red flags, attempted to march on Paris, attacked officers and their quarters, freed prisoners from a detention camp, engaged in rioting, and battled with police and other troops. Order was eventually restored, mainly because 'the whole uprising was essentially a spontaneous protest by desperate and overtired troops rather than a concerted rebellion. Many saw themselves as strikers, not mutineers.' [16] Over 100,000 soldiers were court-martialled and 55 executed, with a good many more shot without sentence. It has been claimed that another 250 were pounded to death by the artillery.

In Austria-Hungary Imperial authority began to break down. With the Russians now out of the war Austro-Hungarian deserters and returning prisoners of war roamed the countryside, plundering as they went, and pillaging wheat-trains. The fall of the Empire was talked about as something inevitable.

A spectre was now haunting Europe – the spectre of Revolution.

In 1918, even as peace negotiations were taking place, revolution broke out in Germany itself, with hundreds of workers' and soldiers' councils springing up all over the country. The German ruling class now resolved to bring the war to an end – no longer to avert defeat, but to prevent revolution. In Italy there was a wave of strikes and factory occupations.

When the war ended soldiers everywhere just wanted to go home. There were mutinies in the American camps in France, mutinies in the British camp at Folkestone, and mutiny among the Canadian soldiers at Rhyl, where order was only restored after six of them had been killed.

And, as if the war hadn't been enough, an influenza epidemic swept the world in 1918/1919 killing some 27 million people, most of them in Africa, India and China. It has been suggested that this epidemic possibly had its origins in the rat-infested trenches of France.[17]

Unrest also came to Great Britain in 1919. Glasgow was paralysed by a general strike, and Belfast saw one of its most intense labour struggles, the strike for a 44 hour week. An overwhelming majority of shipyard men, gas workers and electricity station workers, in search of better working conditions, voted to go on strike. 'A formidable struggle began. Strikers smashed the windows of shops still using gas light and electricity. The trams could not run, cinemas closed, the yards and engineering shops were silent, thousands of linen workers were put out of work, and by the end of the first week bread was running short in the city. Forty-four businesses were brought into the dispute (and) the Belfast Ropeworks were closed down.' [18] The strike was only broken after troops occupied the gasworks and electricity station, and citizens were called upon to work the plants.

And yet all this agitation gradually subsided, and the men who had returned home from the trenches settled back into the needs of civilian life, earning their wages and raising another generation. A generation who would have to follow their fathers' footsteps to France, to fight in an even wider and costlier conflict. For the 'war to end war' had only prepared the ground for the next one.

The Old Order falls asunder – spontaneous demobilisation of the Russian Army, 1917.

Sources

1   Eoin MacNeill, 'The North Began', *An Claidheamh Soluis*, 1 November, 1913.

2   Quoted in *The Irish at the Front*, Michael MacDonagh, Hodder & Stoughton, 1916.

3   Samuel Levenson, *James Connolly - A biography*, Quartet Books, 1977.

4   A.J.P. Taylor, *The First World War*, Penguin Books, 1963.

5   Alistair Horne, 'Verdun and the Somme', in Purnell's *History of the 20th Century*.

6   Brigadier R.J.C. Broadhurst, *Battle of the Somme*, (50th anniversary souvenir booklet).

7   Cyril Falls, *The History of the 36th (Ulster) Division*, McCaw, Stevenson & Orr, 1922.

8   *The War Poets*, The Great Writers Library, Marshall Cavendish, 1988.

9   Lt.-Colonel W.A. Shooter, O.B.E., *Ulster's Part in the Battle of the Somme*, 1966.

10 Philip Orr, *The Road to the Somme*, Blackstaff Press, 1987.

11 H.E.D. Harris, *The Irish Regiments in the First World War*, The Mercier Press, 1968.

12 *Ulster's Tribute to her Fallen Sons*, The Ulster Division Battlefield Memorial Committee.

13 Brigadier A.E.C. Bredin, A History of the Irish Soldier, Century Books, 1987.

14 A.T.Q. Stewart, *The Ulster Crisis*, Faber, 1969.

15 Robert Kee, *Ireland - A History*, Sphere Books, 1982.

16 John Williams, 'The French Army Mutinies', Purnell's *History of the 20th Century*.

17 Barry Turner, 'The Influenza Pandemic', Purnell's *History of the 20th Century*.

18 Jonathan Bardon, *Belfast - An Illustrated History*, Blackstaff Press, 1983.